# The Further Adventures of
# CRAZY JOHN

## by
## A. D. Winans

Second Coming Press

This is a special book issue of *SECOND COMING* magazine and serves as Volume 7, No. 2 of *SECOND COMING.*



Cover photo by Bil Paul

The poems appearing in Part One of this book issue of *SECOND COMING* were first published by Grande Ronde Press as *Crazy John Poems* and by Second Coming Press as *Tales of Crazy John.* The poems in Part Two are previously unpublished.

Library of Congress Catalog Card No.: 79-63967
ISBN: 0-915016-24-9

**SECOND COMING PRESS**
P.O. BOX 31249
SAN FRANCISCO, CA 94131

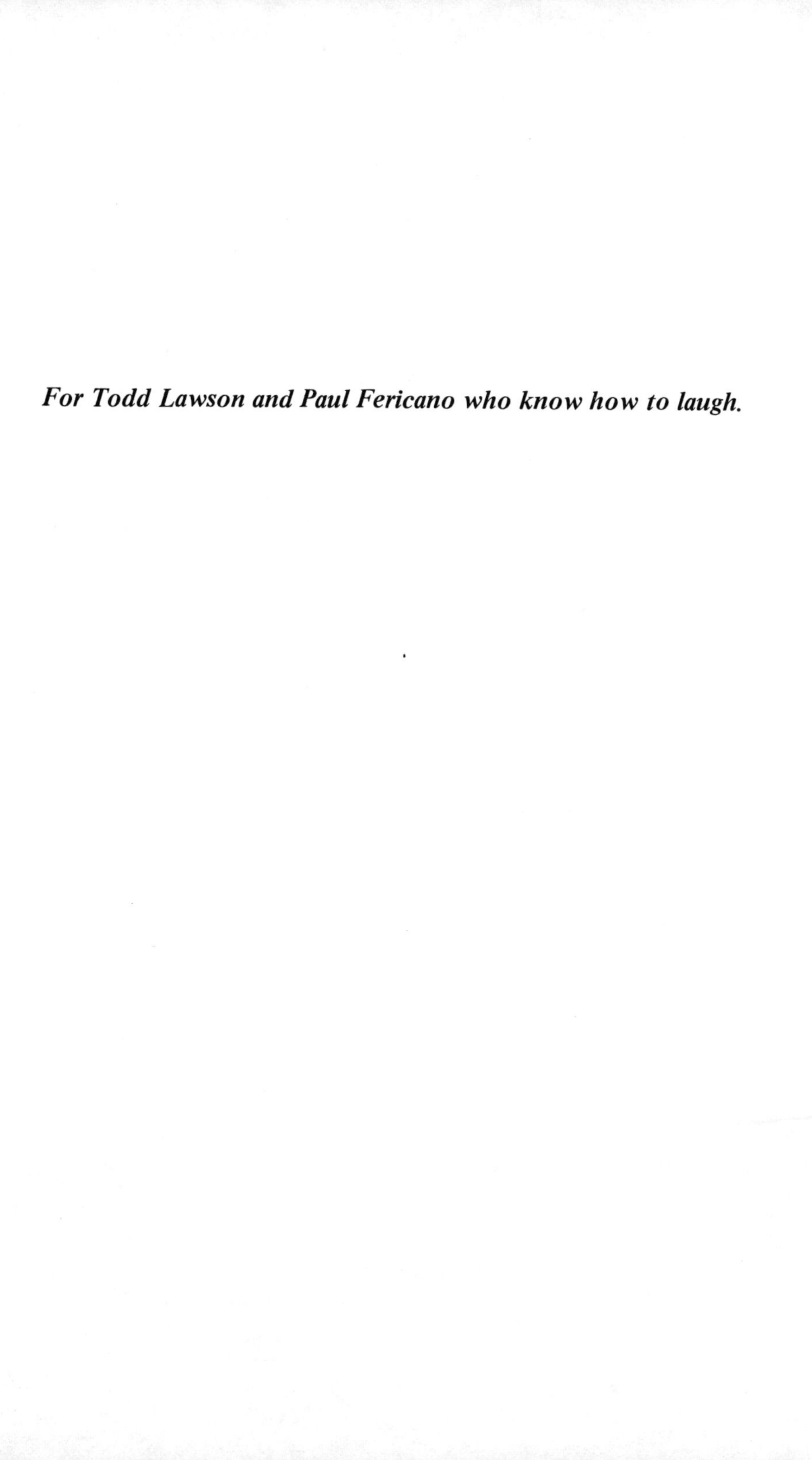

*For Todd Lawson and Paul Fericano who know how to laugh.*

Other Books by A. D. Winans:

CARMEL CLOWNS (Atom Mind Publications)

TALES OF CRAZY JOHN (Second Coming Press)

CRAZY JOHN POEMS (Grande Ronde Press)

ORG MINUS ONE (Scarecrow Books)

NORTH BEACH POEMS (Second Coming Press

STRAWS OF SANITY (Thorp Springs Press)

ALL THE GRAFFITI ON ALL THE BATHROOM WALLS
IN THE WORLD CAN'T HIDE THESE SCARS
(Fallen Angel Press)

A. D. Winans was born in San Francisco, California, and is a graduate of San Francisco State University. He is the Editor/Publisher of Second Coming Magazine/Press, and his work has appeared in over 300 literary journals and anthologies in the U.S., Canada, Australia, New Zealand, England, Germany and Latin America.

He is currently employed by the San Francisco Art Commission, Neighborhood Arts Program, under the Federally financed CETA program.

His work has been acclaimed by many writers, including Charles Bukowski and Jack Micheline. This is his final book on the topic of the mythical character Crazy John.

# One

crazy john was a local poet
of some repute slightly paranoid
with a laugh that never failed to
frighten the establishment and
their highly trained psychiatrists
who recommended that he open
a hotdog stand in downtown san-
francisco but it turned out that
he couldn't handle that either.

it seems he kept on serving
meatless buns sold to him by
overweight nuns threw in
a stalk of celery or two then
stood back in wonder when
the angry crowd yelled:

You must be mad!

crazy john begged me to take him to
see his first baseball game until
i reluctantly agreed and purchased
two tickets to watch the dodgers and
giants knock heads at candlestick
park before a capacity crowd
of over fifty thousand.

in the ninth inning with the score tied
at five and five
crazy john chanted a magic incantation
and i know you'll find this hard to
believe but so help me god
jesus came down off a cloud and
stole homeplate with the giants winning
six to five.

things like that seem to happen when
you're around crazy john.

crazy john bought a used charles atlas
course promising  new found  muscles
at a buck-ninety-eight
all his friends laughed and reacted by
telling him he was as strong as an ox

he countered by moving to bodega bay where
he chased de-frocked monks down
the street shouting:

the madonna has long hair
the madonna has long hair.

crazy john has a friend in bodega bay
they take turns drinking at gino and carlo's
when crazy john's not lying on the floor
drinking irish whiskey from a funnel
his friend can be found in the men's room
trying to set fire to the graffiti on
the wall.

crazy john used to walk
the hills of north dakota wearing
cowboy boots and strumming
a drugstore guitar

late in the evening
he would invite all the town
people to his one room apartment where
he offered to show them old time
roy rogers movies on
the bedroom wall

most everyone laughed except
the sheriff who booked him
for perversion after
he was seen walking nude in
the garden singing folk songs to
wilted flowers who to this day
have never ceased growing.

crazy john used to sell apples on
the waterfront singing haunting
irish hymns

the cop on the beat turned
red
he did not like
the way the songs were sung

they called the paddy wagon
and booked him downtown for
selling without a license

he pled not guilty and offered
the judge an apple core

they gave him thirty days
for bribery.

crazy john got himself a job as an extra in
a hollywood movie being shot on location
in tucson, arizona.

when it came time to cast his part
they found him hiding inside
a fake cactus plant dressed as an
indian.

his only comment was:

"He went that Away."

crazy john used to loiter at the park
handing out used valentines and broken
flowers to passing tourists who cursed him
for his efforts

at night time
he held on tightly to the pillow dreaming
wild flowers and waiting for
the resurrection.

crazy john liked to dance in
the rain
he liked the way it felt and tasted
and the weatherman being somewhat
unpredictable
he invented his own clouds
and sent them high into
the sky but the town people grew
angry considering it an intrusion
on their normal way of life.

so crazy john gave in to
the insistence of the town council
destroyed all but one and moved it
to the woods nearby where
it rained almost continuously
and soon strange flowers began
to grow inch by inch moving silently
toward the city where crazy john
could be seen dancing a raindance
only flowers understood.

crazy john used to sell balloons at
the county zoo laughing with delight
at the sight of the monkeys masturbating
inside their cages.

the frustrated zoo keeper tried
to have him arrested for feeding
peanuts to the bears and trying
to converse with the one-eyed
zebra.

he only laughed tipped his derby hat
and with the help of a friendly
anteater escaped through
a hole leading to china

at least that's the way
crazy john tells it.

crazy john used to draw large crowds
at his yosemite camp site after
the word got around that
he ate a breakfast consisting
of two cactus plants
a lizard
a bald headed eagle and
a prairie dog over easy

after washing it down with good
old mountain dew
he would smile at the masses
belch out loud
sing god bless america and disappear
down the mountain trail riding bare-
back on a grizzly bear scrawling
graffiti on nearby redwood trees.

crazy john used to follow little children
home dressed in a coachman's coat and
a hat full of rainbow feathers

the town people threatened to turn
him into the police for child molesting
he sang them songs in return and danced
outside their doors

they chased him down the block guns
in hand only to find him on top of
the highest rooftop disappearing into
a seeded cloud looking for the right
place to rain at.

crazy john used to drive a yellow cab
cruising the streets of san francisco
clutching a can of rainier ale and
shouting obscenities at shocked nuns
on their way to the confessional

the vice squad thought him
a latent homosexual until
one night a little old lady residing across
the bay rode in on her mechanized wheelchair
and accused him of being the father of
her unborn child

they found him pissing on the stop
sign leading to highway number one
and banished him to the arizona badlands
where he made his fortune selling birth
control pills.

crazy john used to wear a derby hat
to vesuvio's concealed mirrors inside
his vest pocket

at night during the time of the full moon
he practiced morris code off
the bald heads of passing tourists
who reacted as always in blind panic

he joined the first universal church
of truth and offered them
immortality.

the lights flicker on and off at
crazy john's house

the heat has been turned off
P-G & E spends many long hours
sending him overdue bills

you can find him at home snuggled
up between the covers dreaming
the impossible.

crazy john gave in to the unemployment offices
insistent demands and took a job as a conductor
on the skunk train in not so far off mendocino
where he spent the better part of the day chasing
frightened passengers down the aisle trying to
punch holes in their hands and gather tongues
for baggage checks

they kicked him off in reno where
he lost his fortune at keno and found
himself in the black mountains of dakota panning
for fools gold and selling used road maps to
german stuka pilots looking for lost dreams.

on nights of the full moon
crazy john would sit for
many long hours eying
his empty 16 oz mug waiting
for the closing hour when
he would raise his hand
demand absolute silence
and delight the crowd by
causing the malt liquor
to rise up the side of
the glass topped off with
just the proper head.

they say crazy john is mad
because he claims to converse
with the ancients grabs strange
girls off the street and trys to
sell them his peripheral vision.

sometimes on a warm
summer night people come
from far off to watch
him gather fruits and nuts at
the local farmer's market

but it's been many years since
i've seen him perform a miracle.

he claims that
he's waiting for
the holy ghost to come out
of hiding.

they locked crazy john up in
a padded cell where three
doctors took notes with unbelieving
eyes watching him create butterflies
from alphabetical blocks then turn
into a frog forced to devour
his creation in order to survive.

in the morning when
he changed back again.

he had three doctors for
company.

# Two

released from the nut house
crazy john took the court's advice
stopped off at the state department
of rehabilitation and signed up for
a course in fingerprint identification
walking the streets for clues insisting
he was the direct descendant of
sherlock holmes that
the answer to life lay hidden in
the crematory.

the cops not buying it and remembering
him from an old mug shot hauled him before
the magistrate who sent him back to
the home for the criminally insane where
he took refuge in the piano playing
old caruso songs reciting bukowski by
day and mc kuen by night.

the old folks dancing in the halls
the echo reaching the ad-min office
who ordered him removed taken back
to court where he was given
a one way ticket to reno nevada.

all but the crippled street hobo
avoiding the look in his eyes.

they found crazy john a job telling
fortunes in a san mateo county
gypsy parlor
the first time they crossed
his palm with silver
he got up and left

"wait"
the elderly woman complained
"where are you going?"

to seek my fortune he smiled
disappearing into
the crystal ball reappearing
five years later in
a lifeboat salvaged from
the titanic

crazy john used to hang out at
the waterfront bent over
the harsh lights
his pen scribbling frantic messages
into the night rewriting
the doubts of his childhood
he frightened them all especially
the seamen who distrusted him most
one moment threatening them with
the gangplank
the next turning into a gentle
tugboat captain causing chaos
at riordan's bar where
he took up residence in the men's room
trading graffiti with drunken irish
peanut vendors pretending they were
the new generation flushing their
dreams down the toilet
like proper businessmen searching
their suits for a flaw

crazy john enrolled at
the state university signed
up for the track team intent
on winning a position on
the u.s. olympic team

at the height of the pole vault
he lost his pants and was
declared ineligible by
the judge after
he chased him into
the locker room through
the showers leaving disguised as
a patient on a make-shift
stretcher

kicked out of school
for unsportsman like conduct
he laughed tipped his derby hat
to the board of trustees and created
his own olympics running through
the streets of san francisco carrying
a flaming torch inviting
rod mc kuen to preside over
the first ever world poetry
olympics.

crazy john took a job
at the post office dressed
like the hero of his dreams
a cowboy hat and a pair
of six guns strapped to
his side

popping valium to see
the evening through tapping
out invisible images in
old mail trucks and letter alleys
the watchful supervisors acting
the part of keystone cops with
reprimands for warrants

counseled for insubordination
and a bad attitude
he reported one last time disguised
as the lone ranger leaving
a silver bullet in the confused
tour superintendent's hand then
changing into a magician
one last trick left up
his sleeve exiting
like charlie chaplin
hat and cane dancing in
the wind

crazy john showed up in russia
one leap year dressed as a frog
popping valium and blaming
the croaking of frogs for
his lack of sleep

jumped in the deep end of
the swimming pool reappeared in
the children's end bobbing
for apples before returning to
eureka california to take
the job of state game warden
vowing to reappear every
four years secretly plotting
the taking of
the mad czar's dreams.

crazy john got arrested for
the umpteenth time threatened
with shock treatments at
napa state hospital after
an apple cheeked police officer
fresh out of the police academy
noticed him in the park building
sandcastles with three year
old children the next moment
standing in the lurky shadows pretending
he was humphrey bogart hands in
his trench coat pocket reciting
lines from woody allen's
"play it again sam."

the cops flipping out because
they were only familiar with
starsky and hutch.

crazy john was voted
the unofficial mayor
of north beach by
the last of
the hippie generation
took to sitting around
washington square picking
his toes
and laughing a lot
and when asked why
said:

"only the shadow knows."

crazy john was found waltzing alone
in the long abandoned avalon ballroom
warned to leave by the night watchman
he joined him in the fox trot
the two step
the ali shuffle
the old rope-a-dope itself
his eyes two candles lighting
up the night

in the morning they found the guard
laying exhausted on the floor
crazy john smiling still dancing
around the room accompanied by
the music of long forgotten orchestras
playing delicately in the wings

crazy john took up with
a notorious san francisco
drag queen took
a job as a gypsy fortune teller
reading tea leaves at
a chinese funeral home

parting the shadows with
a wave of his hand
he led the funeral procession
merrily down the street complete
with an imported new orleans
black jazz band

the white shirted black suited
cadillac undertakers left
spellbound empty handed blue
eyed and furious.

crazy john used to wander lovers lane dressed
as a security guard dropping counterfeit
coins into empty parking meters while counseling
nymphomaniacs on the high rate of V.D. offering
discount rubber sheathed vibrators at low cost
until he was placed under surveillance by
the state police who lost him less than twenty-
four hours later when he disappeared behind
the locked doors of a monastery who later
nominated him for sainthood

crazy john went back-packing stopped
off at a roadside cafe and played
the jukebox long into the short
of three irish coffees
got a fourth one free when
he told the aging bartender
it was his birthday then bought
a round for the house disappearing
disguised as a birthday cake
made three quick wishes then
left dressed in a party hat
the waitress waving a sparkler
at the shadow of his backpack
sitting on the mountainside
huddled with the snow
two hound dogs joining him
in a song to the moon

crazy john attended a female liberation
convention disguised as vogue magazine
spreading around nude photos of
norman mailer

the delegates in an uproar marching
madly to the music of
john philip sousa

watching in disbelief as
he came out of hiding draped in
the garb of a matador displaying
a penis a yard wide taking in
the womens cheers
he ran from lap to lap preaching
of equal rights and the clap
the crowd yelling
"ole — ole" — as
he disappeared down the aisle
and into the streets taking with
him the state delegates
of alabama, new york and california
on a never ending excursion into
a life of perversion

repairing shattered egos
with flattery and strapped on
rented dildoes

he dropped them off at
the y.m.c.a.
a fatigued weight lifter strutting
off like a peacock

a man among a sea
of eunuchs.

crazy john was introduced to
the wonders of opium by
a chinese seaman at
the harbor inn

caught wandering the docks
a mad twinkle in his eye
he was sent to mendocino
state hospital
put on a diet of librium and
four valiums a day
he broke out one summer night
accompanied by a former indian
scout who took him to the top
of a mountain where
he consulted with Rip Van Winkle
Cardinal Spellman and old man
Oral Roberts who betrayed
him by turning him over to
the junta who made
him a civil servant only
to have him escape again reappear
in Salina Kansas disguised as
a wise man selling balloons to
children and telling tales
of the world series to
old war heroes bent eagerly
over coal iron stoves

crazy john was excommunicated from
the church for preaching that
jesus christ was really
cecil b. de mille
thrown out of congress for claiming
that abe lincoln was really john
wilkes booth in disguise
forced to leave in disgrace
he left for australia in search
of a mate who might bear him a son
who would perpetuate
the impossible